Gabby Douglas

ABDO
Publishing Company

by **Sarah Tieck**

Big Buddy BOOKS
Buddy Bios

Published by ABDO Publishing Company, PO Box 398166, Minneapolis, Minnesota 55439.

Copyright © 2013 by Abdo Consulting Group, Inc. International copyrights reserved in all countries. No part of this book may be reproduced in any form without written permission from the publisher. Big Buddy Books™ is a trademark and logo of ABDO Publishing Company.

Printed in the United States of America, North Mankato, Minnesota.
092012
012013

 PRINTED ON RECYCLED PAPER

Coordinating Series Editor: Rochelle Baltzer
Contributing Editors: Megan M. Gunderson, Marcia Zappa
Graphic Design: Maria Hosley
Cover Photograph: *Getty Images*: EMMANUEL DUNAND/AFP.
Interior Photographs/Illustrations: *AP Photo*: Charles Rex Arbogast (p. 10), Mark Baker, File (p. 17), Gregory Bull (p. 5), Jason DeCrow/Invision (p. 27), Matt Dunham (p. 19), Virginian-Pilot, Steve Earley (p. 8), Scott Gardner, CP (p. 17), Rex Features via AP Images (p. 17), Amy Sancetta (p. 10), Jonathan Short (p. 24); *Getty Images*: David Eulitt/Kansas City Star/MCT via Getty Images (p. 13), Scott Halleran/Getty Images for Kelloggs (p. 7), Streeter Lecka (p. 23), Ronald Martinez (p. 15), Margaret Norton/NBC/NBCU Photo Bank via Getty Images (p. 29), Ryan Pierse (p. 25), Cameron Spencer (p. 21).

Cataloging-in-Publication Data

Tieck, Sarah.
  Gabby Douglas: historic Olympic champion / Sarah Tieck.
    p. cm. -- (Big buddy biographies)
  ISBN 978-1-61783-748-7
  1. Douglas, Gabby, 1995- --United States--Biography--Juvenile literature. 2. Women gymnasts--United States--Biography--Juvenile literature. 3. Gymnastics for women--History--Juvenile literature. I. Title.
  794.44/092--dc22
    [B]
                              2012946487

Gabby Douglas

Contents

Olympic Star

Gabby Douglas is a famous American gymnast. She has won events around the world.

In 2012, Gabby won two gold **medals** at the Summer Olympics. One was for the individual all-around event. Gabby was the first African-American gymnast to win this event!

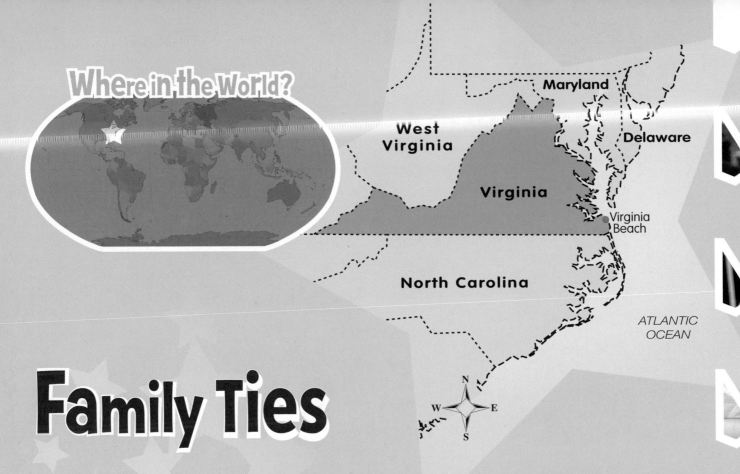

Where in the World?

Maryland

West Virginia

Delaware

Virginia

Virginia Beach

North Carolina

ATLANTIC OCEAN

Family Ties

Gabby was born in Virginia Beach, Virginia, on December 31, 1995. Her full name is Gabrielle Christina Victoria Douglas.

Gabby's parents are Natalie Hawkins and Timothy Douglas. Her older sisters are Arielle and Joyelle. Her older brother is Jonathan.

USA

Kellogg's
CORN FLAKES

The Original & Best

SINCE 1906

GABBY DOUGLAS

CEREAL
NET WT 12 OZ (340g)

LONDON 2012 LONDON

Gabby's family often attends her events.

People in Virginia Beach painted a wall honoring Gabby.

Early Years

Gabby grew up in Virginia Beach. When she was just three, her sister Arielle taught her to do a cartwheel. Soon, Gabby learned to do this with one hand!

At age six, Gabby started gymnastics training. Before long, she was winning events.

When Gabby was about nine, her father left to serve in the military. Life changed for Gabby and her brother and sisters. She didn't see her dad much anymore. Her mom worked hard to support the family.

Dominique Dawes won Olympic medals in the 1990s. Growing up, Gabby looked up to Dominique.

Liang is known for his coaching skill. He also trained Olympic gymnast Shawn Johnson.

Starting Out

Gabby had a **goal** to **compete** in the Olympics. She knew she needed different training to improve her skills. So, she asked her mom if she could work with a new **coach**.

When Gabby was 14, she moved to West Des Moines, Iowa. There, she worked with Liang Chow. Liang is a well-known gymnastics coach. He pushed Gabby to improve. Soon, she was competing at a higher level.

In Iowa, Gabby lived with a host family. She moved in with Travis and Missy Parton and their four daughters. They took care of her. Training made it hard for Gabby to attend regular school. So, she was homeschooled.

Gabby says Missy is like a mom to her. At the Olympics, Missy (*left*) and Gabby's mother (*center*) cheered together.

Big Dreams

Gabby trained hard. She **competed** at many gymnastics events. Then, she earned a spot on the 2011 US World **Championship** Team. She helped her team win the gold **medal**!

Gabby became known for her skill on the uneven bars. People thought she was talented enough to do well at the Olympics!

Gabby is sometimes called "the Flying Squirrel." This is because she can get very high when she lets go of the uneven bars.

The Olympic Games

The Olympic Games are a famous worldwide sports event. The games happen every two years. They change between the Summer Olympics and the Winter Olympics.

People from around the world **compete** to win Olympic events. First-place winners receive gold **medals**. Silver medals are given to second-place winners. And, third-place winners receive bronze medals.

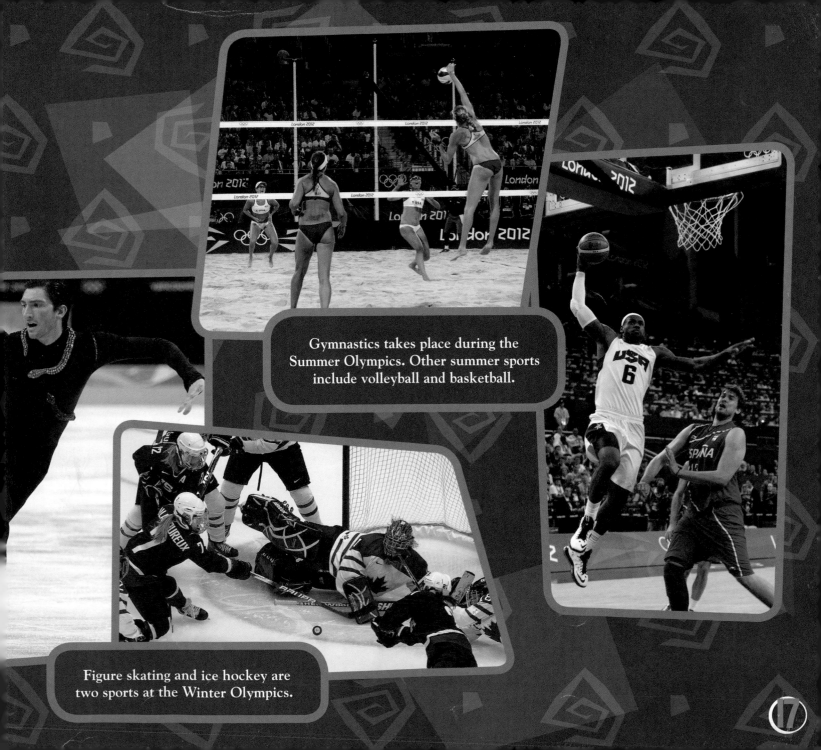

Gymnastics takes place during the Summer Olympics. Other summer sports include volleyball and basketball.

Figure skating and ice hockey are two sports at the Winter Olympics.

17

The Fab Five

In 2012, Gabby reached her **goal** of **competing** in the Olympics! She had scored very well at the trials. So, she was the only one sure to have a spot on the team. Gabby traveled to London, England, for the Olympics.

London 2012

Gabby was one of five gymnasts on Team USA. Her teammates were McKayla Maroney, Aly Raisman, Kyla Ross, and Jordyn Wieber.

At the women's team event, Team USA earned a gold **medal**. Soon, they were known as "the Fab Five" and "the Fierce Five." People were very excited by their success!

Jordyn, Gabby, McKayla, Aly, and Kyla (*left to right*) were given their medals in a ceremony.

Olympic Champion

After the team event, Gabby did the individual all-around event. She won a gold medal! She was the first African-American gymnast to do this. She was very proud.

At the Olympic Games, Gabby was honored for her skills.

The balance beam and
the uneven bars were the next events. Gabby gave her
best efforts. She didn't win any more **medals**. But she
was grateful for the experience. And she was proud of
what she had done.

People admired how Gabby pushed through her mistakes and challenges.

Outside the Gym

Gabby's gymnastics training and events keep her busy. But when she has free time, she likes to spend it with family and friends. She also enjoys knitting and reading.

After their Olympic win, the Fierce Five visited the Empire State Building. It was lit in red, white, and blue to honor Team USA.

Buzz

After the 2012 Olympics, Gabby looked forward to some time off. She was excited to rest and spend time with her family and their dogs.

Fans hope she will take part in the 2016 Summer Olympics. They are excited to see what's next for Gabby Douglas!

Gabby appeared with First Lady Michelle Obama on *The Tonight Show with Jay Leno.*

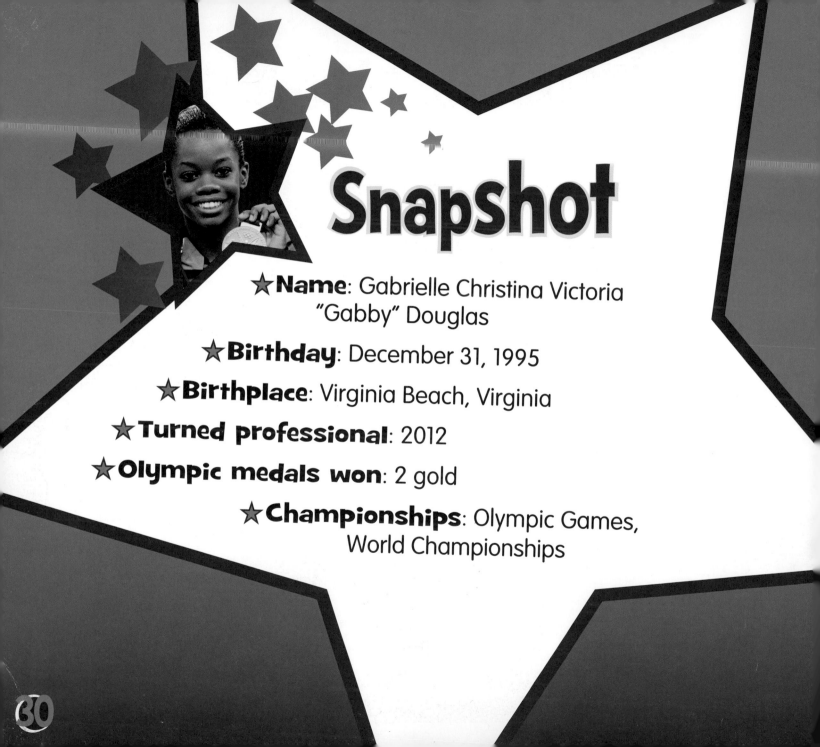

Snapshot

★**Name**: Gabrielle Christina Victoria "Gabby" Douglas

★**Birthday**: December 31, 1995

★**Birthplace**: Virginia Beach, Virginia

★**Turned professional**: 2012

★**Olympic medals won**: 2 gold

★**Championships**: Olympic Games, World Championships

Important Words

championship a game, a match, or a race held to find a first-place winner.

coach someone who teaches or trains a person or a group on a certain subject or skill.

competition (kahm-puh-TIH-shuhn) a contest between two or more persons or groups. To compete is to take part in a competition.

goal something that a person works to reach or complete.

medal an award for success.

Web Sites

To learn more about Gabby Douglas, visit ABDO Publishing Company online. Web sites about Gabby Douglas are featured on our Book Links page. These links are routinely monitored and updated to provide the most current information available.

www.abdopublishing.com

Index